Home

Sofia Willhauk

Copyright © 2023 Sofia Willhauk

All writing is allowed to be shared by readers across all social media platforms as long as the author is credited.
Sofia Willhauk / @sofiswelt_
All rights reserved. No part of this publication may be reproduced, distributed or transmitted in any form or by any means without prior written permission from the author.
Cover design © 2023 Lilli Brittner
Illustration © 2023 Filloreta Alitaj / @that.fillo

ISBN: 9798376907528

To Michelle.

And to Lisbon.

PROLOGUE

This collection of poems is my fleeting attempt to get to the bottom of our zeitgeist,
to grasp its essence, trying to capture it in imperfect rhymes.
A mosaic of pebbles, as colorful and intricate as life itself.
Snapshots of noisy summer nights and lonely autumn evenings.
The testament of a profound yet distant longing to arrive without knowing where exactly.
My poems are about searching, finding, and losing. About beauty in pain and its healing power.
About what makes us feel alive most, uniting yet dividing us at once. About discovery and denial, anticipation and wanderlust, magnificence, and shame. About the courage to break new ground and the fear, which is its constant companion. About acceptance, farewell and reunion. About love, loss, and fear. About truth always being colored by the lenses through which we see the world.
Home testifies a journey of healing, my personal fallacy to believe I understood life and love and the humbling pain in this naive erring, accompanied by the ironic wink of life itself, indicating that all my thinking will not lead to understanding in the end. I hope you will find yourself in some of these snapshots, in the midst of my lines, a hidden part of you.

CONTENTS

i   crescendo   11

ii   ecstasy   39

iii   descensus ad inferos   81

iv   catharsis   129

"The feelings that hurt most,
the emotions that sting most,
are those that are absurd
the longing for impossible things,
precisely because they are impossible,
nostalgia for what never was,
the desire for what could have been,
regret over not being someone else,
dissatisfaction with the world's existence.
All these half-tones of the soul's consciousness
create a raw landscape within us,
a sun eternally setting on what we are."

Fernando Pessoa

i crescendo

on days like today
i tend to look back
turning around
i'm baffled how quick
time flew by in a blink
without quarrel indeed
deprived me of mine
loneliness' doubts
all the more left it for
colors and bliss
new faces
old secrets
so many questions
wrapped daintily in poems

prelude
—

i am everything
i am nothing
i am now

all is right
all is wrong
all good takes time

be good
stay honest to yourself
work hard
choose not the easy
but the uneven path
stand straight for all you treasure
if people you care for
are falling astray
don't hesitate
to help them back on their way
together you'll get farther
and as you do know best
together is richer in abundance
deeper in every substance
than just by yourself

while always seeking truth
allow yourself to question
what truth really means
keep your mind widely open
learn from what startles you
in unforeseen surprises
magic may find you

choose insight over judgment
avoid harming for you
as well as your surrounding
defy your temptation
to help everybody
not each one is able
to see it as love

use your beautiful mind
claim your body's mettle
remember how current
evokes within rest

of all things however
laugh more than you dare
rekindle fires
with your warmth again

joy is what heals us
it's our lives' precious light
every quarrel
in kindness unites
don't take yourself seriously
we're all here to learn
life holds so much pleasure
have the courage
open your heart
trust its innate wisdom
follow its spark

namaste
—

are we rewriting history
witnessing a change in times
or will all dwell in poetry
a single breath of loneliness

my gaze off wanders wordlessly
how placid beauty seems to lie
sun dyes our world colorfully
silence unites everything

in early summer
i like to lie on
freshly mown grass
longingly looking to the sky
counting planes
wondering who is inside
so happy that we found a way
to bypass continents
playing time itself a trick
reversing overnight
its rules and zones so quickly

today i don't see any planes
sky above me clear and blue
the world is standing still
nobody knows
how long

2020
—

i want you to know
you're not walking alone

when you pass by
plenty abides
life continues to try
sometimes
i wish you would stay
stride more slowly
linger a while
rest a little
pause for a blink
evaporate just not so quickly

i know you must go
because you can't help it

one day
you will take me
in your arms i will see
where you always vanish
you take me with you
we will disappear
you will no longer wander
all by yourself

i'm wondering quietly
what will remain
when you and i go

raindrops
—

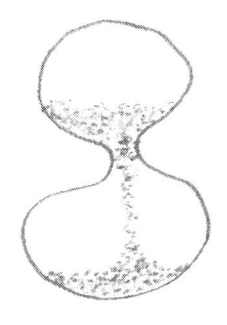

your eyes are filled
with questions which i cannot hear
what is it that you're running from
abashed i try
look at my feet
forcing a smile
a random chance
unspoken i reply
in truth however
which i will never let leak through
i am afraid to fall for you
again alive and full of youth
mistaking lust for something pure
yet soon already
numbness in my solar plexus
when i hear no more from you
once again my closeness
apparently too close for you
your smell your touch
you do not know how much
i miss you in the darkness
of my loneliness
trying to find
what isn't there
wondering what makes me stay
waiting for you to take courage
rip off your masks
facing your fears
trust you and me

it seems you only seem to see me
when i am getting up
to leave

pattern recognition
—

before you left
you kissed me gently
for the first time
just very briefly
almost an incident
as if your lips touching mine
equals a casualty in time
knowing each other
for a while
today we left
something behind

softly warm lips
beautiful kiss
always enjoyed
but never missed
intimacy between us
i'm wondering if
this kiss might
have meant
a you and me
maybe

and yet i know
at least for me
maybe
means no

tepid
—

each of your dreams
will come true
when you pause and listen close
what your inner voice
tells you

search for meaning
fight for beauty
only you know
where to find it

listen carefully
it is within you
i know
you know

truth

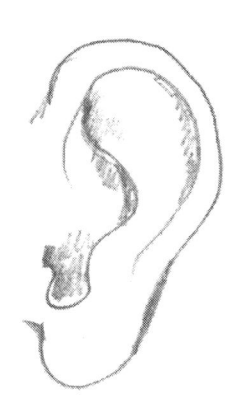

you know me better
than i admit
notice before me
what i try to hide

while i still
slightly dazed
believe the story
i keep telling myself
you don't need much
to unveil truth's
bittersweet sentiment
behind my tired lies

sometimes your questions
yet sometimes
nothing but wary silence
is shaking me awake

jannika
—

for the first time
i realize
what flows
deeply through my veins
i begin to understand
why i am the way i am

seeing you in other people
apparently grown up
deep in their hearts however children
of youth deprived
over the changing
of regimes

ussr

sometimes i crave
nothing but silence
urgently needing to hear my voice

withdrawing
summoning
truth and insight

realizing way too soon
how much it's you
i desire
beating my doors in storm like manner
demanding me to leave my den
reminding me that life requires
to be explored amongst the living
not in-between my syllables

corset
—

we do not know each other
distance across time and space
complicated our embrace
holding on to my heart's spell
i believe our paths will melt
one day in a vivid place

his blood is running
through our veins
you're always with him
while all i have
are blurry memories
polaroids in black and white
testimony of a past live
not enough time
for a young child
nor a young father

we do not know each other
but i know too well
what my heart tells
and how much
i find myself
loving you
today already

little sister
—

early morning in the south
a fleeting moment in between
a quick espresso on the run
already leaving
suddenly i turn around
slowing down i feel
sun's rays tickling my skin
still young already shining
in its fullest glory
i could stay a few days more
or maybe even longer

is home a place
if so just one
or rather a sense of belonging
a vague emotion
even a person

late evening
back in almada
steep stairs
way down
along the river
ponto final
bino waving from afar
"olá! where have you been that long?"
"at home, visiting family."
"and now you are back at home here!"
nodding smilingly i sigh
home is not just anywhere
yet not tied
to a single place

quest
—

having a muted conversation
which you seem bravely to avoid
i hear my voice rattling in circles
between maybe and perhaps

quickly becoming fond of you
mistaking oblique for parallel
still wondering
was i too honest
revealing my desire
easily giving in to yours
was i too much or just too little

no
i wore no masks
was my true self
whoever that might be
if that was
not enough
or even too much for you
then we should never
aim for more

modern love

thinking nothing
feeling less
somehow fine
yet not myself
sometimes there
then lost again
overrun by stimuli
always somewhere
in between

days pass by
i wonder
where did my
time fly

too much of days like these
and soon i will not be
able to tell
who i am and what's my name

where i am going
what i intend
staggering loosely
fragmented mind
without direction
lost in translation

burnout
—

you came later to my life
since then never left my side
on all paths i chose as mine
your love always was my light
cozy blanket in cold times
stretched out hand
never too tired
seldomly angry
always wisely understanding
finding right words
patient and gentle
not afraid of
asking questions

you are my reason for many things
even though i noticed late

dad
—

ephemeral
unquestioning
for every state
my island of tranquility
patient white sheets
you don't forget
what escapes my memory
remind me of eternity

yesterday about to fade
tomorrow not quite yet awake
you capture moments
keep them safe
while i distort reality
you expose truth's fragility
you are me and i am you
your body streaming in black blood
from underneath my fingertips
and don't i hear myself
i'm listening to you

paper

maybe you were
not ready at the time
maybe you thought
we were not aligned

our intercourse
taught me
what should not
will not thrive

everything falls
just as it must
i trust the dots
my future holds
firmly grounded
in the past

steve jobs
—

i feel for you
nothing but pure gratitude
strolling through your colored alleys
my distant home
atlantic's shores

independent lightness
pure joy
spring's smile
always so alive

still here
yet painting my farewell
where will life take me next
will i return
not having answers to these questions
i feel i will in time
wondering today already
will i appear just in new clothes
or as a fairly transformed woman
with unknown longing
new dreams and bold desires
back to the known
or daring to embark
on novel paths
this time

lisboa
—

while i always go away
you firmly stay
i know you will remain
peacefully waiting
in warm familiarity
when sooner than later
i find myself
needing you
again

rock solid
—

if i must make a choice
it wouldn't take me long
around us were no whirlwind
never too much noise
two cups of steaming tea
for hours we could talk
for more than seven years
you have always been
my favorite new beginning
my brightest day in spring
curious explorer
deep waters float within
your even deeper veins
delicate map of wonders
under an even softer skin

no matter what
you were
you always will remain
my rising and my setting sun
simultaneously

love of my life

every place so beautiful
dipped in violet and green
early summer young and keen
pleasantly warm
and not yet burning
feelings tingling
fears still quiet
everything so promising
at this time i've often been
daring and courageous

jacaranda
—

flipping through marie's love life
inspired by her romances
pleasantly daring
a smirk escapes my mind
want to give in
to night's adventures
floating around
forgetting time
did i not recently decide
i want somebody to abide
someone wanting to build a life
yearning to share my life
growing together with a man
whose soul shares my aspiration
for depth as well as lightness

i had my wild and restless nights
i left them far and long behind
they never were the potion
in which my molecules
caught light

tinder stories
—

ii ecstasy

an encounter
at the junction
of two lives

at the same time
in the same place
nothing but a happenstance
reason wisely says
yet i don't trust a word it tells

amber green
—

"friends
stunning stories
mind blowing conversations
hikes and adventures
life loving people
that is exactly what i am looking for as well."

isn't it what we all look for
a home within a heart
inside an unknown soul
the breeze of familiarity
a promising prelude
a beautiful beginning

"seems a good match then.
where are you?"

hola
—

"i ran away
from love
my whole life
until i realized
to love means to decide."

i wonder why
i thought
with me
your fear
is going to resign
your heart will open
refuse to run away this time
decide for me
for us

i raise my eyebrows
sweetly lying
"but why
fleeing from love?
never would i."

i wonder why
i thought
i could conquer my anxiety
this time
decide for you
for us

fear of commitment
—

a day in tardy may
lisbone principe real
widely smiling
i watch the scene of crime
in front of me
people outside
some bold some shy
my youth mature
not missing anyone
as usual
can hardly wait
what's yet to come
a summer young
playful with joy
infects us all
lisbon glowing purple green
to its contrast i appear
fully in black
long skirt short top
my hair tied up
worn out boots
carrying so much life in their old soles
deeply familiar with dirty floors
oh where already have they danced
how often lost their way

vividly smiling to myself
how can i be so blessed

my display lights
you have arrived
daringly i catch your eye
you rather shy
unable to hold my sight

you both seem nice
so absolutely not my type
life laughs and pulls my leg
within no time

vividly smiling to myself
how can i be so blessed

our night still young
our conversations running deep
we laugh we cry we are naive
meeting each other
without the need of masks
unadorned in honesty
i am amazed how sometimes
out of a sudden beauty ignites
life's a surprise
one step aside
can change the tide
side effects of an open mind
felipe waiting for the car
i'm quickly jumping to the bar
turning around
i find you right in front of me
i cannot leave nor hide
you take my hand and kiss me
demandingly
yet at the same time very gently
a shudder breaks through me
serenity covered in black abates
moments pass by yet it feels
as if time actually stands still
when your gaze finds mine

pinky promise
—

your breakup fresh
our conversation
opened wounds
that deeply bleed inside

awkward smiles
between
pressed lips
avoided gazes

i can't do that
it just blurts out
"if you need to let it out
it's okay and i'm here
i'll cry with you if you need me."
wondering you look at me
"i will do that, sofi, thank you."

not everyone is able to
meet pain
showing it openly
to oneself and strangers
we're all great protagonists
in our own theater
well experienced players
you knew to refrain from
such behavior

peanut butter
—

"i have a friend
he loves his girl
she betrays him
yet they seem happy
i should not know
i can't decide what's the right call
what would you do?"

"i would try to fight for truth.
always waking up the slave
déjame que te cuente."

socrates going for a walk
gracefully enjoying
fresh air surrounding him
stretching his nose into the sun
greeting the birds flying above

sunk in sleep by the wayside
he discovers a slave
floating in his deepest dream world
his face transmitting utmost peace
believing he is free
he loves it
he seems happy

socrates wonders
what to do
should he wake him up
tell him the truth
expose his illusory freedom
or let him dream his happy lie
what will serve him most in life?

socrates' dilemma
—

three friends
one journey
the constant flow of time
solely deciding
who goes and who abides
loudly remaining silent
our hearts beating
one rhyme

your gaze wanders the distance
green spreads in front of us
finding a piece of home
familiar scenery
on a foreign ground
your eyes are filled with sadness
your heart bleeds out in salt
while i see your tears falling
i'm sad she never will

i hope this burning pain
will bring you clarity
time working its magic
will heal your heart again
so freshly broken it
needs love and peace and rest
a phoenix has to burn
to rise back from its ashes

laurel
—

life plays its game so quickly
i'm hardly keeping up
dark then light again
hours lapse away
night beguiles the day
sun takes its revenge
dancing with each other
forró in whirlwind
the world around us blurry
i feel so alive

time lapse
—

cascais is still half asleep
mild raindrops falling evenly
from a tired veil
after turgid days and never-ending nights
gray silence hanging in the clouds
seems to be just
what we all direly need

while i am writing in the kitchen
my thoughts drifting far away
my past weeks' loneliness forgotten
seemingly more than years ago
i feel so good around you
getting familiar to your voice
quiet and smoky always warm
more and more robbing my mind
triggering a storm inside

out of the sudden a woman enters
interrupting our melting
within my daydream phantasies
her somewhat tired looking skin
encompassing intense blue eyes
a stunning beauty she must have been
coming back to portugal
fairly long she was not ready to return
vainly trying to avoid a place
where she lost something

burning with curiosity
i can't help asking nosy
"why particular this beach?"
smiling wistfully she tells me
about a tango festival
almost a decade ago
her eyes go waxy
she isn't with me anymore
she is there
at the bright plaza
on top of lisbon's city hills
dancing argentine tango
emitting passion pride and glory
moving sensual like a swan
her capital conjuncts all colors
mature in youth she takes no no
a handsome man holding her tightly
his hand resting on her waistline
he's whispering a secret quietly
"you must come to
a beach called guincho
i'll wait for you
where waves are
melting in with sand."

her voice is breaking
all i can do is guess
in her intense blue eyes
i see so many questions
hope falling astray
a whole world
and its pain

wayra
—

"did you know that mozart
could hear what he saw?
the quiet gray of rain
made him beyond sad.
he wrote so to his sister
on a rainy day."

ludwig
—

i fall in love so easily
but probably quite rarely
yet if
whole worlds
are merging
deep inside of me
quickly i
tend to forget
what i wanted before
believing sometimes even
not to want it anymore
nothing appears difficult
everything feels possible
and yet
i want to keep my mind
i am quite fine
do i really want to compromise
just to be by his side

helena
—

while i pretend to be asleep
i feel a burning on my skin
your gaze is warm
your breath goes deep
i hear your fears talk in your sleep
quickly doubts became so loud
knowing secretly already
this may bring us to our knees
distance is your greatest worry
mine however your confusion
which at the same time flatters me
i turned your head
and showed you love
without any venom

fire
—

"look at me."
same air we breathe
you inhale what's leaving me
giving in
losing myself
feeling something rare and pure
i haven't known you long in time
yet is this how i feel

chemistry
—

five nights no sleep
in dawn our eyes meet tiredly
nevertheless widely awake
interwoven
intertwined
we are breaking
our last night
sharing each other
becoming one
your gaze holds mine
my body trembles in excitement
as it never has before
your warmth next to mine
chest moving up and down
your breath suspends the silence
where have you been
in all these years
it doesn't matter
now you are here

skin

quickly our last night passes by
new light already born outside
a fresh day on its way to rise
saying nothing
we both know
a moment brief in time
blink of an eye
saying goodbye
to someone
whom we did not miss
in our busy lives

not knowing if
not asking when
only heartbeats
disrupting silence

saudade
—

do you believe
life has a plan
or is it all
mere happenstance

after the last week
i can barely tell
it caught and threw me
through the air
laughed at my plans
cheerfully yelled
"spread your wings and fly, my child!
this is what i made you for."
i didn't have the time so far
still just floating
above clouds
beneath the sun
not even trying to find answers
not feeling a necessity
to understand
since i can't do so anyway

while i crisscross the universe
my lungs are filled with beauty
i believe strongly life writes great stories
paints them in the brightest colors
accentuates with poetry
mischievously listens to our fears
hiding behind a corner grins
"whether by chance or by design?
spontaneously i decide
and will hold warm for you
what you need most to thrive."

waymaker
—

an early morning
a taxi to the airport
big suitcase and two backpacks
a very normal couple
on its way to fly

however we are everything
but a normal couple
two strangers on a journey
familiar after hours

my life five days ago
looked so very different
what are five days
on the span of a life

yet i have never seen us
as an elusive casualty
not at the first sight and after
you never were a stranger
special from the beginning
you felt like home to me
an old piece of my soul
of which i never knew
that i missed it before

zrh, sfo
—

exhausted
i recognize
sleepless nights
endless days
fatigue and
paralysis
noisy questions
many people
little time
always show me
what lasts and
what abides

without you
i would not survive

all that i am
is also you
our bond a cure
constantly guarding
from the first sight
counting seven years together
from the first hi
side by side

for every flight
you book my seat
not asking me
you check me in

waiting and
smiling when i arrive
always seeing me first
waving and calling
"hello my person!"
hugging each other
quietly and deeply
every time it's
as if it was yesterday
and almost too long

looking at me
deep in my eyes
i don't need to speak
you're reading my mind

no words

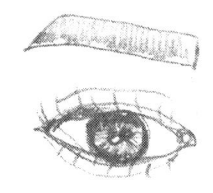

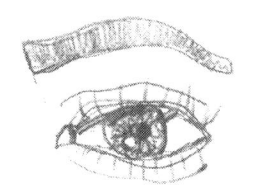

we sit down
i start to tell you
still not really understanding

your smile is like
a melody of
boundless joy
dwelling in melancholy

you see
i am about to fall
for someone who lives far away
whom i still do not know at all
at the same time you recognize
the utmost warm glow of my eyes
what i tell you
warms your heart too

when two souls
are so close
when i am you
and you are me
we'll always keep
encountering a dreaming thrall

waking up
or letting sleep
lying down right next to me
dreaming together deeply

symbiosis
—

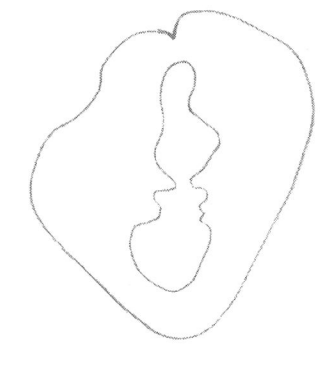

"i miss you."
after no time
"i miss you too
i love this photograph of you
capturing unvarnished truth
your beauty's essence
shivering pleasure
raw and pure."

between the lines
our young love
doesn't need many words
flourishing in silence

"i want to see this smile again
feeling what i have never felt
only longed for
not knowing it
existed."

snapshot
—

thinking about you
i barely understand
knowing to process in letters
impossible to me
our explosion happened
beyond suddenly
my head is shaking
so are my legs
my body craves yours
distance massive
i barely know you yet
days joyful
nights intense
my lungs are filled with light
and pleasures' restless breaths

you will have changed my life forever
only i don't know so yet

domino
—

any door in front of you
will open if you choose
colorful adventures
your life is in the starting blocks
just about to begin

abundance
—

mom smiles cheekily at me
"are you in love?"
rebelliously i sigh
"not yet."
michelle's voice behind the corner
"it won't take her so much longer!"
nodding slowly i confess
"it will not take me much longer."

i'm blown away
by life's sophisticated yarning
our beautiful encounter
the happenstance itself

as if my ladies hear
the voices in my head
they're blurting out together
"there is no happenstance."
i do not disagree
this non-occurrence feels
too healthy and enchanting
to be a random chance

kitchen talks
—

you taught me
what truly matters in our lives
breaking rules
questioning norms
instead of calmly compromising
not only to enjoy my time
moreover to survive
immovably trusting
god knows what he does
laughing at our earthy plans
boundlessly loving us
you showed me
what true love really is
and how it always wins
with your thick skull
driving reason
and far too often me
bluntly out of mind
laughing constantly
accomplishing all which
reason can only dream of
stealing hearts
you shifted borders
learned a new language
for your great love
never forgot your own
you taught me
everything is possible
if i only want
the people i brought home
you loved as much as i
i am beyond grateful
to have you in my life

mom
—

a fresh breeze strokes
over my bare and sun kissed shoulders
june's wind playing with my curls

matilda bites her lip
beaming at me
questions to ask she can't resist
"when will you see him?"
"vamos a ver."
playing cool
i'm telling her
continuing my monologue
we shared
very special moments
only time knows what future holds
if it is meant to be it will
if not

i swallow

my heart is filled
with nothing but mere gratitude
for the first time in my whole life
i feel attraction united
with lightness in intimacy

healthy
—

i begin to understand
why everything before you
should not have been
i see how much
i missed
when i thought
i didn't

missing piece
—

there is so much
i want to show you
my favorite village in the alps
lisbon's most hidden corners
my home
south africa
and more

i want to
see the world with you
encounter beautiful and true

without knowing
who you are
naively not asking you
i just planned my life with you

quick
—

the sun is crisp
it joyful glints
while dancing happily
on tejo's surface
i am in our favorite park
counting all the clouds above
cotton candy frozen up
on the red bridge in front of me
cars in slow-motion passing by
i'm looking to the other side
and see us laughing back in time
your eyes meet mine
my mind still fights
my body doesn't even try

the big red bridge
far over on your side
spreads its tiles
below a different sky
paving a way across pacific's realm
i'm wondering
if there
cars also in slow motion pass
clouds in the sky
bear semblance to
cotton candy caught in time
and if you're smiling while this sight
catches the corner of your eye
reminiscing our time
in early summer
portugal

ponte 25 de abril
—

we are a dance of
dazzling colors
noisy nights
delightful daylight
lisbon makes it very easy
for us to fall deep for each other

while moments pass
all reason fades
we find ourselves under a spell
endless possibilities
a summer
circling in infinity

santo antónio
—

adventures tickling my nose
my heartbeat races
what a month
a year so full of magic colors
yet seems it truly just to start
tears in my eyes
i'm wondering
where is this journey taking me
what is a month
all or nothing
suddenly everything
seems easy
vast abundance
beauty and excitement
simultaneously

priklyucheniye
—

with you
i tasted life
just a small sip
a gentle bite
it tasted like
a potpourri
of never-ending summer nights
a melody intense yet quiet
beethoven's tender sadness
meeting mozart's vivid vibes
above the salty ocean sky
flowers open up as kites
stolen sleep
and sugar highs
chocolate pancakes
at midnight
conversations running high
laughter ringing dark and dry
latin charm
and russian pride
math and language
sparkling vibes
deep and rich
yet fear is lurking
from behind

crushing distance
long goodbyes
close your eyes
who rolls the dice
gentle kisses
cheeky smiles
you and i
we broke the nights
sleepy mornings
tender touch
we forget
what distance means
gap too big for us to stretch
past keeps throwing doubts around
closing my eyes
i still deny
what i already know inside

churros
—

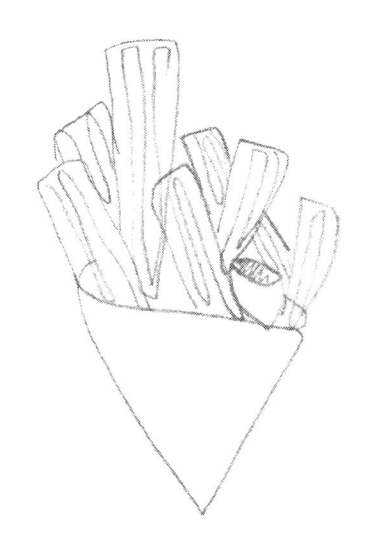

what i feel with you
doesn't seem real
scarily beautiful indeed
restraining an old worn fear
to lose myself within a feeling
i'm wondering
if it must be
because somehow
without knowing you for long
it just feels like my soul does so
i listen deeply while you speak
seeing in you what you don't see
i think that you are missing
someone like me
in your so fast paced
dance with life

no airbag
—

i am an early morning's sunray
pleasantly warm
but not yet burning
completely free
so without worries
i don't quite know
where i am drawn to next and when
no matter where i end
i'm going to shine there
maybe i am not awake
caught in a dream
and yet i feel
my truest self
rejecting unshaded singularity
embracing a sea of possibilities
not really questioning the now
carrying so much love in me
sun's warmth deep in my heart
wind's whisper in my eyes
everything is beautiful
just as it is right now

summer
—

sun is bowing a farewell
in the corner of my eye
i see you
leaving the cab
wearing old jeans and a light shirt
backpack just over one shoulder
can't grasp your gaze
wearing a perfect poker face
sunglasses covering your eyes
i cannot help
my lips curl up
into a smile of joy
you're here again
for the third time within a month
i bite my lip
can someone pinch me
you're coming closer
tousled hair and a cool grin
what seems your normal
still so intangible to me
my life compared to yours
predictable and regular
"welcome back
must feel like home."
your covered eyes looking for mine
holding my gaze for a long time
they wander off to find tiles of a bridge
you've come to cross more often
than you had in mind
barely audible you sigh
"home. that's what it actually feels like."

ah-lee-yahz
—

do you remember
how we
were running
to the bridge

it was
just time
running
thereafter

marco
—

iii descensus ad inferos

are you running away from me
are you running away from
are you running away
are you running
are you

maybe

you are
you are running
you are running out
you are running out of sleep

forest gump
—

what is a thought
when does it start
when is it calm
when is it loud
when is it me
who owns the thought
and when do i
obey its call

what is a thought
how can it have
so much power over me

sam harris
—

the more we fall
the deeper our claws are tearing
my words like salt
your silence poison
in our unhealed old worn wounds

lightness changed its place with worry
claim bleakly abandoned humor
silence long between the lines
cold air fills the room inside
bitterly your doubts reside
my fears desperately loud
we hurt each other
without intention
unheard we feel
misunderstood

suddenly it's more than oceans
separating our worlds

did we not just yesterday
lie together
skin to skin
our hearts
one beat
how can this be

nightmare
—

i don't feel often anymore
living life somewhat composed
between deadlines and appointments
too busy functioning
not enough time
to lose in yearning

meeting you reminded me
of how i one day used to feel
burning ice
rain drops evaporating
melting with sun
a firework of flowers
universe in abundance
beauty in pain
heat in heaven
oasis in a desert

probably this is why
out of nowhere
my fears again awoke to life
doubts disguised as reason
ensnaring my bare heart
swerving away from meaning
avoiding deep encounter

like iron rusts in oxygen
you infused my life with air
beautifully scary
quicker than usual
my solid walls gave in

these walls
when were they build
by whom designed

a voice seeming so similar
yet not quite mine
eagerly tries to warn me
"don't play with unknown fire
you'll burn your heart
following its desire."

beneath also one
seeming more like mine
asks carefully
"but isn't fire also light?"

troy
—

hiding behind a veil of smiles
i hope no one sees the light
that extinguished in my eyes

i am trying not to cry
wrapping myself in a thin cloth
of understanding and acceptance
stoically striving
not to crumble
accepting numbness

i know i tried
my words were not enough
you did not hear them
i must let go
to not lose more
looking straight into pain's face
allowing my wounded soul
to heal again

dust
—

watch out
next time
look closely
listen to silence
read between lines
be more on guard
ask yourself
if you trust
who appears in front of you
or if you only see
what you wish to find

lucifer
—

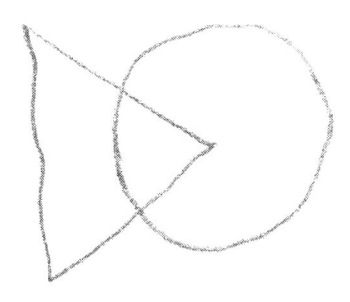

any pain
which you live through
makes you who you are
helps you understand your life
paves the way ahead of you
shows you what you truly need
reveals reality

you will laugh
you will cry
you will rise
you will fall down
you are alive
you do your best
you have loved
opened your heart
you've hurt yourself
and you've hurt others

it all shall pass
you have lost nothing
love is infinite
breathe and trust
you will get through it
you will not break
you will learn
you will heal
you will come home

jesus
—

"no dear, i do not understand
we always have a choice
we can decide for ourselves."

i reckon sadly
laure has right to be in doubt
you came to stumble very fast
just after a few nights apart
you appeared so very cluttered
your voice tense
signals confusing
"i am not her."
i'm telling you
a plaster that refused to glue
a wound she left behind
too deep for a new life
you are not ready
you love me
and you are sorry
hoping i believe

mar y sol
—

if we were knitted another way
then this would not be us
and if we were a movie
you'd be with me right now

if we were a writer's romance
there would be a happy end
faithful love and courage
would be back in trend

then you and i would have
the guts to take the step
admitting that we are
missing someone special

unfortunately we are
more than just a book
more than just a story
written by my quill

i think it is called life
it seems intricate
both hearts
have lost their way
passion went astray

maybe it was me
who just got it wrong
saw what wasn't there
thought that we were more

between us silent walls
fear disguised as reason
but in truth anxiety
jumping to conclusions

our lives flying by quickly
between noisy nights
free and yet alone

i wonder if you remember
the smell of my skin
my fingertips on yours
the color of my iris
when i used to give in
i wonder if you still hear me
moaning in your dreams

the desire to believe in us
lacked courage in the end
maybe it was just
a naive poet's dream

perfectly imperfect
—

a new beginning
summer's first breath
fresh rain on a hot day
a lightning strike in the mundane
sun's early smile just after dawn

our paths evoked in chance
you felt like future
in our midst i found
worlds to discover

yet needs tomorrow
now in distance and vicinity
our today however
staggers off the path
lurches like befuddled

i am no longer sure
whether we are still
going with the wind
and also not much longer
if my love can win
against your fears

dead end
—

did i too quickly sh
not looking close e
seeing only what i w
ignoring the distortio
nights of silence
absent answers
boulevard of question n
soon of shattered hearts
distance out of a sudden
appears to be too far

i would be myself again
straightforward and honest
maybe even more so
i would help you understand
that silence is my venom
my protracted trauma
i would reveal my cards
they are who i am
if i choose to hide them
i also hide myself

no pokerface
—

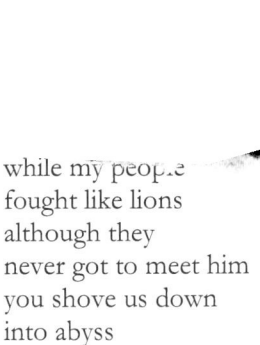

while my people
fought like lions
although they
never got to meet him
you shove us down
into abyss

you and i know
and maybe even he
did so

i have forgiven you
hurt people are
hurting people
after all

wounds
—

you chose silent withdrawal
i cannot hold it against you
talking your greatest weakness
that of most
you never hid it
but also never tried
to fight the quiet

we all choose
invisibility as a way out
embarrassed
looking away
somewhat ashamed
pretending to forget
dressing in smiles
avoiding conflicts
keeping alive
unresolved circles

shame

waking up
embracing
this new day ahead of me
choosing understanding
salving myself
in humbling acceptance

trying my best
yet suddenly
without a warning
i break apart
burst into burning tears again
scolding myself
for my fragility
desperate about
what seems to be
your ignorance
little boy's fear
not trusting love
ghost from your past

caught in my sadness
i'm failing greatly
to recall empathy

i breathe
remind myself
so early
you've lost your faith in love
your parents busy
on their own journey
reason has always been
protecting you from scars

mike travis
—

it seems
you have moved on
why do i
find myself incapable
to just let go
finding
all the indications
i believe to miss

chinese whispers
—

while i was taught
to tell the truth
no matter what
no halfway through
come what may
not to camouflage myself
behind my own hypocrisy
reveal my lies against all hurdles

you have learned
to smile politely
to be demurely silent
avoiding conflicts when you can
remaining calm and quiet
a solemn trait
yet also one that made you
bury anger deep in you
never allowing your emotions
to ever show themselves

always protecting
the ones you love
by staying silent
i still don't understand
since when exactly
does truth vanish
by not being said

you do not only hurt the ones
who truly crave to understand you
you deprive yourself of meaning
hiding behind a portrait
not painted by your hand
close to a life in matrix
what would neo say

deep rooted fear
devours your soul like ivy light
while you seek home
and deep connection
you're running from it
at the same time

american dream
—

you let go
yet i still struggle to move on
trapped in a standstill
holding on to hope
slowly icing up my heart
my brain asks anxiously
why do you do this to yourself

i don't know
how you have been
which path you chose
how you feel and how it goes
all i can do is wondering

meeting my inner child
my pride gives in
i hope you grow through what we were
i hope you'll find just what you need
if you don't suffer anymore
it only warms my ice-cold heart

i don't want you to suffer
torture yourself with guilt
i want you to find joy
everlasting peace
without fear and doubts
falling for someone
aware of your worth
recalling our story
melting of two worlds

intention behavior gap
—

my breath is failing
my heartbeat becomes frantic
my stomach cramps
tears flood my eyes
not asking for permission

i slowly wonder
that i still have some left

so fast
so clueless
so without ifs and buts
i locked you in my heart
without waiting
without asking
if this was also what you wanted
it happened just like that
after a few days only

naked

why are people standing
in their own happiness
in their own way
isn't that crazy
why are we
i thought that you and me
were different
i thought we didn't want to hurt
each other
not standing in our ways
rather walk together
dancing through night and day
i was so sure
we both wanted
the same
that i got this so wrong
will always remain
a mystery
to me

last morning
—

how can
my world keep turning
while my heart remains frozen
how can a stranger
so fast
become a someone
and out of a sudden
a nobody

vertiginous
—

i liked you quickly
i admit that very freely
not hiding what i used to feel
our time together promising
out of a sudden
fear and doubts frozen in silence
a well-known sin of modern love
somehow just not something
that i would ever have expected
from you
a mature man
who saw the world
and has met life

amygdala
—

how can i believe
to love a man
not really knowing
who he is

you were right
love is a choice
i wonder
when i decided
and today also why

uterus

when people ask me later
why i fell the way i fell

when my wounds build walls
i find myself cursing you for yours

when my heart freezes unforgetting
an early summer's melody
intense yet short-lived symphony
seized only by melancholy

i want to shut my eyes widely
able to reminisce

i fell in love with
warmth and kindness
soft skin and voice
in a warm gaze
always awake
and never tired

i fell in love with
peace and quiet
bold dreams and
glowing aspirations
big questions
an even deeper mind
in the gold shine of amber eyes
their radiance when you were laughing
sharing secrets and cariños
often just observing quietly

in a curious pioneer
who found between my thighs
a secret long unknown to me

i fell in love with
a being full of wonder
creative soul
beautiful heart
five languages resembling one
in boundless curiosity
the joy of a young boy
in a grown man
who's mere gaze
softened me
in seconds

ponto final
—

it takes me years to realize
how i am fractured deep inside
a loss experienced too young
back then still a little girl
ever since tightly holding on
catching a familiar feeling
confusing it with something real

i look for men akin to you
torture myself in these old shoes
not trusting anyone will stay
avoiding closeness
run away
before you hurt me
i will hurt you
before you leave me
i will leave you
vain loneliness
an accurate
self-fulfilling prophecy
to heal i need
to travel back
rewrite the story in my heart
you've been so young
a dad and yet
yourself a child
a lonely man
whose love abruptly died
my words are not enough
to describe what you must've felt
when your world broke apart
as well

divorce
—

goodbye
take care
just yesterday
it seems
and yet
you feel
a world away

i wonder
how you are
if you can sleep
if the wind
roaring on my side
soothes your melancholy
if it calms your heart
caresses your soul
if on the paths
you chose
faith is your companion

fonte
—

an unclean cut
will always be
a maybe
hanging by a thread
almost alive
and yet not quite
swallowing hope's
bittersweet poison
i'm falling
for the wrong belief
there will always be
more time

maybe means no
why does a part of me
still hope
that love will heal
what we could not
be braver than
your fear
to fall for me
and mine
to lose myself
therein

yet
maybe hurts
maybe is coward
maybe is hoping
without colors
maybe is sun
behind a glass

liberalism
—

two steps forward
one step back
two moons together
one apart
the sky outside
looks sad to me
lonely and gray
unpromising
am i still missing you
or am i just losing my mind
freely choosing agony
asking too much of myself
isn't my emptiness allowed
what else could i feel

today feels more like
one step forward
two steps back
my heart in vacuum
its beats suppressed

growing pains
—

a dead bird rests
on the floor right next to me
scarlet shines its still wet blood
the tiles in red are smeared

what might its death stand for
coincidence and nothing more
a sudden loss of love
a storm is coming closer

did something die with it
that held me blindly tied
for which i chose to give in
my faith in love
so genuine yet naive

my dead friend did not
see the windowpane
flew against it in a dive
still hurting i would sign
though my heart resigns

looking down to my companion
its blood has not yet dried
eyes widely open
it doesn't move a dime

requiem
—

on better days
i do not feel the weight
of having lost us
due to our different ways

on these same days
i am shocked how
easily memories tend to blur
close souls give way
as if the bruises on our hearts
equal frail tracks on mellow sand
so lightly blown away by wind

on my sad days
my heart's mute howls
equal atlantic's current
in which i slowly seem to drown
swimming against it
vainly seeking solid ground
while mother nature tirelessly
draws me back
into her restless waters

i can't escape my longing
wondering
what we might have become

polyphemus
—

i collapse
gasping for air
another flood of burning salt
finds its way out of my eyes
how many times more
why

folding my hands
before my chest
quavering
on my knees
i'm praying for salvation

"dear god i know too well
i am not a faithful child
say grace much too rarely
however when
i seem unable
to bear it anymore
otherwise stumbling in a spell
scientific knowledge can't explain
create my truth
by what is widely recognized
always forget to pay tribute
to my own human ignorance
if you wish
equal our ways
and if not
i am begging you
deprive me of this mania
give me back to myself
help me to heal
find your lost child."

anemia
—

i don't remember when
i began to wake up
while the world around me
found itself in dreams
everything still dark outside
in the middle of the night
i am opening my eyes
starring in the gloom for hours
turning from my left to right
capitulating
getting up

checkmate
weary and tired i think about you
remembering how you have told me
you were not sleeping long for years
waking up
your mind in circles
five hours do you suffice
you have more time than those
who give way to rest

when we met
you were tired
i ask myself
how long already

wherever you might be today
i hope you are in peace
within night's gloomy silence
yet moreover in you
i truly hope that soon
i can sleep again too

sleepwalking
—

sitting in the evening sun
observing poseidon's game
waves building up and breaking down
sometimes arriving gently
sometimes wildly racing
seemingly never getting tired
continuously striving
always just in time
to kiss the shore goodbye

my thoughts are painting circles
slipping from my consciousness
embarking on a journey
a tale of you and me
we do not longer speak
and if then much too quietly
our words caught in politeness
i bite my lip in silence
i miss you
although i'd never show you

where did we lose each other
does this where have a location
when love stumbles
does it get up again

from many drops of water
an ocean was created

everyday life
—

reality and poetry
rarely run in parallels
relationships are complicated
scripts written incompletely
truth often remains hidden
its essence lost incessantly

sometimes love seems to end too soon
yet sometimes way too late

not black and white
—

we did not lose each other
we never looked for us
i couldn't give you time
you just couldn't trust

i think what hurts you most
is that you truly tried
not to break my heart
unable to speak
you stole its spark
confused me with your past
let off the chain
my limbic siren
which in exchange
equally unintentionally
imposed great pain on you

we always have a choice
a question of free will
is moral integral
can i choose what i want
categorically
i don't know

cracked open
i can finally
breathe

schopenhauer
—

sometimes i wonder
if i'm too honest for a world
that seems to be in love with lies
repressing truth politely

where love does not resemble
a place of warmth and confidence
but is confused with unclear signals
addiction
chase and lust

lovingly and warmly
my mother's gaze rests tenderly
on her wounded child
"my too good girl
old pains' youth
so wise and yet so blind
paying the price of virtues
which we have lost in pride."

i still believe
our world
would be better off
if people strived
to see the good
spread warmth and truth
there cannot be
too many
too honest
and too soft

coriolanus
—

maybe a stranger
remains a stranger after all
although you never were to me
i saw what i knew
feeling familiarity
i thought to know you better
than i ever could
didn't see the burden
you took on in youth

a stranger is not easy
and neither were you

gladwell
—

hurt i believe
we had not much in common
feeling blind and naive
i seem to buy into my grief
in light we often shared
such distant views
on fundamental things

trauma
—

"take care of
your heart
that tender soul
of yours."

i promise you
i will take care
of my prefrontal cortex
my neurons and my axons
i will heal my traumas
feed my microbiome
disrobe my distortions

making sure
my gorgeous heart
beats strongly
belonging to my soul
open to the world

ember
—

some hurt
by words
yet some by silence
inflicting wounds
triggering violence
caught up in fear
our minds on fire
running in circles
sleepless and tired

i'm sorry that i hurt you
it was the last thing
that i have ever wanted

incongruence
—

i do not hold you
i know i can't
but i will never be too far
if you will ever need me

lipstick
—

iv catharsis

when we first met
you said
"we have all the time there is."
we became friends
despite rumors and great distance
preserved long what friendship needs

at some point we lost
what always made us who we were
i closed the door
left a gap open
you let it fall into the lock
not out of anger
rather sober reason
so long already
we were running blindly
back and forth
catching what died
ages ago

mostly i think
it is good the way it is
i envy your cold temper
to find the means to finally let go
no longer hold on to a pale shadow
whose light we once have been
goodbyes have never been my strength
today i miss
my once best friend

blue les paul
—

it hurts me
to see
how you daily
choose old chains
decide to wear
what has been
imposed on you

to be
who you are not
putting on a mask
which is not yours
blindly searching meaning
fleeing away from feelings
a patrimony of strength
what does it mean to be a man
a fate defined by genitals
denied vulnerability
everything under control
fainting smiles
suppressing joy
fitting in over belonging
when all fades
you remain lonely

masculinity
shaped by performance
signs of weakness
out of question
your soul's value measured only
by success and solid figures
greatness not a form of virtue
rather physical appearance
is the last one to decide
what we as manly consecrate

intimacy calls for
an odyssey of change
every man of our time
must learn to feel again

i'm sorry
that i didn't see
what the whole time
obviously lay
in front of me

the boy in the club
—

how can we be
so much alike
and yet so different
at the same time
i see you suffering
behind a mask of anger
loneliness caught in silence
quickly appears as violence

when did you learn
to be alone
not needing anyone
cutting everybody off
when did you choose
to be too strong

maybe true strength
means cancelation
allowing weakness
accepting help
forgiving people
letting love in
dancing together
imperfectly
rather than
stumbling perfectly
alone

feminism
—

it helps me to
lose myself in letters
finding in past all that
had helped me many times

invoking healing and resilience
in a pain far from today
seeing
no matter
how much it burned
it never chose to stay

life always stole my sorrows
wind always brought new air

i know that time will seal
also this wound of mine

the next time
when love comes
i wish that love will stay

maybe i was not ready
although i thought i'd been

time
—

i see a girl in front of me
a cheeky grin curls up her lip
beaming playfully at me
her eyes are shining happily
is she still missing him
not much longer it seems
the places they have been to
a cloud of memories
blurred colors
faded odors
illusion of the past
have they ever been here
or was it all her dream

phoenix
—

"i loved my thirties
they were my favorite years
a vivid time
i knew exactly who i was
what is important and remains
i'd learned to love
and to let go
i found myself
i fell in love
with my own
light and shadow equally
with each sunrise inhaling
motley wonders this life offers
for every sunset grateful
ready to begin."

katalin
—

suddenly you appeared
not asking questions
you were just here
brightening my day

terminos
—

with you
i was ready
to settle down
quite naturally
i became calm
stopped looking around

while i am healing
my true self back
my spark returning
a motley butterfly again
sipping life's sweet nectar
smelling many pleasant flowers
stealing their secrets in abundance
i remember very dimly
an almost childlike tummy tingling
my radiance when i saw you in front of me
in young june so surprisingly
my longing when you had to leave
our midnight laughter in the kitchen
your dark brown eyes
resting on my skin

favorite flower
—

i am grateful
to be who i am
i know today
i am a sum of many
who were before me
some are long gone
others remained
i wonder
who will stay
until the end

richard david precht
—

slow wake up
early morning
cold shower
fresh clothes
hot ginger
warm words
nostalgic poetry
beautiful honesty
pain and its healing power
ephemeral melody of life
three years almost
you walk with me
through mountain peaks
and valleys
to distant worlds
deep canyons
in spring meadows
wide as narrow
you say fulfilled
my mind bubbles with liveliness
after all this time
you truly are my anchor
you found with me
answers to suffering
in my deepest rooms
and secrets hidden in between
i am forever grateful
for you holding on to me
always understanding
patient beyond limits

the red couch
—

farewell forever
or farewell for a while
do we have to lose first
to see what abides
missing you again today
i don't want time
i don't want forgetting
i don't want goodbye

schizophrenic
—

how can i miss
what i don't know
unknowingly holding on
to worn out truth
dogged on old paths
didn't come far
grasping my heart
i spread my wings

departure
—

writing these lines
with a sad smile
in a café
in alcantara
early july
seeing us there
on wooden stairs
with sean and palu
if someone would've told me then
i'll miss you like i do today
i would've laughed
shaking my head

i do not know
if we will ever meet again
nor when
yet still
i'd always choose
it all again
my skirt and top
the book
the bar
i'd steal your look
and take your heart
i'd give you love
which you so fear
but deeply crave

we all learn pretty well
how to be strong alone
not needing anyone
individuals all along

but we fail mercilessly
giving each other time and space
showing vulnerability
giving love
what it needs to thrive

we run away
before it hurts
we're building walls
as if forgotten
that light cannot shine through
behind them secretly we suffer
outwardly we are doing well

sadly i'm smiling to myself
being alive means
feeling everything

santana
—

you are the artist among us
in every soul around
you find a hidden universe
possibilities and wonder
beauty and depth you see
wherever your gaze wanders

i admit freely
i fell for you in just an instant
didn't mind staying for good
not afraid to lose my mind
fire in every cell of mine
i still don't have the words
to tell what you have been to me

tenderly solacing my soul
still looking for its lost companion
taming my lack of apprehension
holding tightly my bare heart
still refusing to let go
defying my commands
listening to an ebbing song
failing to forget
what it knows
displacing

maybe related souls
are just not meant to stay
serve only as a mirror
show us what we avoid
reveal the truth
tear down old walls
find our shadows
steal our sleep
break our hearts
burst open we recall
to breathe

i have forgiven us
as long as my heart beats
i will always choose love

promise
—

"did i confuse
cold feet with reason
choking our young love's throat
hurt him before
he could've hurt me?"

"if you then so did he
how many times did you
slam the door
decide to leave
ran away
made us believe
we've grown apart
there is no common ground
everything was different now
no future to be found?
yet never have we let
your fear cut our solid bond
as wild as your storm raged
the waves always calmed down
and you returned back home."

you always understood
deeply loved my wounds
a sky full of stars
we're all full of scars
they are our integral
and we are each other's

friendship
—

my decision
against all reason
to wait
giving
this young love
the air it needs
embracing us in memory
during the cold of winter

meanwhile giving
myself time
to heal and
not to hurry

trust
—

always on the lookout
perpetually on the go
movement is your steadiness
consistency your curse
you belong to journey
its fever is the melody
floating through your veins

i on the other hand
equal an old pine
i come to stay
strike roots through trust
open up slowly
reliability is my incense
my words never mere dust

your soul's home
poseidon's salt
in width you find intimacy
your whole life you're collecting
new stories and old secrets
seeking truth in meaning
moving on when ease
slowly begins to bleach

when your soul touched mine
you left something behind
a spark of heavy longing
which i stumble to grasp
how can i miss somebody
who never meant to last

air and water
—

this feeling early in the morning
the sun just waking up itself
stretching its rays
looking forward to the day
unfolding right in front of me
whispering its secrets gently

oh life you rascal
i think now i understand
what you were saying all along
i must find my own world
mine and not just one
not my place in his home
last summer
broke apart not me
but the old vase
in which i held myself
caught tirelessly

free

what could be more beautiful
than to wake up smiling
early in the morning
a smile that just belongs to me
embraces life
illuminates the world
recalls bold dreams
believes in miracles

happy
—

my head is spinning
infinitely
finally it's whirling
not around you
anymore

wild
—

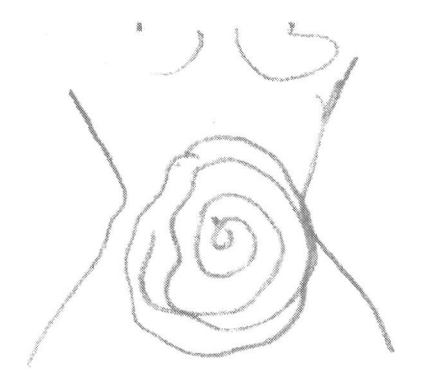

magnolia's withered blossoms
lie tired in the hay
early spring's graceful beauty
she shies away from chill

autumn's motley garment
returns little by little
many a bird sing
i still hear today
most of them are however
already far away

against all the birds
in autumn i return
here i rest my wings
peace refills my lungs

through silence i can hear
my own voice very clearly
feel rather than think
become myself again

homeward
—

i am with another man
feeling indeed
somehow okay
at least not more in burning pain
of course not how i felt with you
swallowing this bitter truth
a question scratching
below my skin
will i ever feel again

and yet it seems to do me good
enveloped by affection
sheltered in arms
brave enough to hold
what your silence left broken
not asking questions
my grief remains my secret

i close my eyes
try to believe
that i like this
while his arm
slowly gets heavy
embrace too tight
a shudder creeping up
a question scratching
below my skin
will i ever feel again

not you
—

one year passed by
i wonder where i can find
what yesterday
i thought of all the time

appointments
worries
unwritten stories
all the words remained unsaid
all of what we have never dared
my time with you never enough
mistakes so crucial after all
answers i kept looking for
not understanding what we were
pressure always to do justice
fulfill the claim i made myself
my fear to waste time in the process
chasing blindly just the vain

suddenly all of this
seems so unimportant
out of place and almost pale
i hope i'm back on the right path
far away from a life i thought i knew
or even something i called so
i feel close to myself again
much closer than i was
when i thought
i would like to be part of your world
a planet whose air soaked all my oxygen
which i gave away freely
unable to see how your world simply
did not have enough room for me
thereby so often hoped
something was there when it was not

one year passed by
i found myself surrounded
by beautiful abundance

falling in love so easily
without buts and without fear
with my whole heart
without my mind
with nature's beauty
indian ocean's shimmering blue
with blowing wind and new beginnings
with utmost honesty and friendship
courage and greatness quiet spaces
with writing poems rhyming letters
with a wide land
its motley landscape
with its sad history
scars hardly more than black and white
apartheit's breath still holding tight
to people's hearts
confine their minds

i fell in love
with asking questions
looking for truth
with all its shadows
with breaking nights
on kitchen instead of dancing floors
with rooibos tea
hour long deep talks
with changing plans
rewriting future
abandon courtesy and sorrows
with losing every sense of time
not measuring our life in seconds
but in mere happiness instead

one year later
i do not wish
you were with me anymore
i carry you no longer
know there was not enough space for me
in your busy life
which with my effervescent striving
i only more disorganized
i would lie saying
i don't think about you anymore
certainly i do sometimes
a fleeting echo strikes my mind
i shyly smile just like a child
i hope you're fine
hearing your breath just back in time
your voice so tired in the night
your hand warmly on my thigh
it's in your eyes where i discovered
what always used to remain silent
your never-ending faith in me
knowing that i will succeed
"you are a world of miracles
don't be afraid to sail the sea
always keep steering against wind
sometimes you have to leave
to find your path again
who said plans will remain
and who that dreams will not
who said mistakes are not important
and who determines good and bad
stand in your truth
take care of you."

i do not hear your words
in dark brown eyes
i only see the many places
valleys harboring oceans
i see beauty
a bright mind

one year passed by
i saw written in light
what yesterday i as important sanctified

table mountain
—

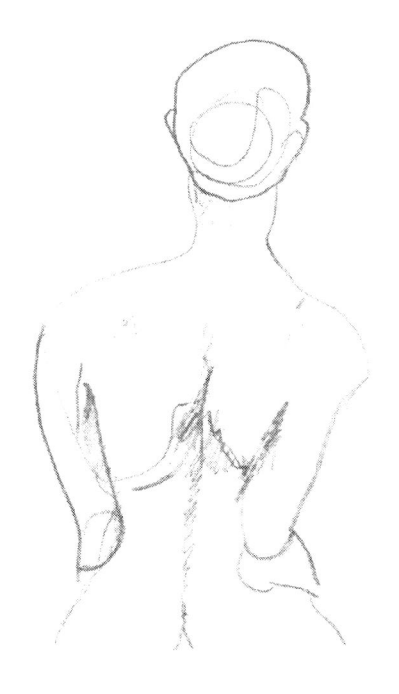

today about
to say goodbye
yet before only night abides
burning beauty dyes the sky
shiva dancing in its heights
showing us what makes our lives
filling our world with light
igniting fires
on the horizon
gently opening our eyes
demanding us to pause and sigh

beauty to be found
in mother nature's
everlasting countenance
in your eyes
and in mine
in this first
already vanished
momentum

all this remains
while we pass by
like raindrops
vanish in
mother earth
always returning
to the sky

magic
—

would you recognize me
if i'd randomly stroll by
across the street
at a café
in front of me
a cup of tea
worn book in one
a pencil in the other hand
mischievously grinning
engrossed in thoughts
caught between lines
would you know immediately
or would you need some time

somehow i'm pretty sure
you would know instantly

blonde
—

the days are getting shorter
white snow covers the land

now and then
i believe
to miss you as a friend
yet i slowly understand
my feeling can't be quite right
love that ought to end too soon
is love that never got a chance
and thus never began

the days are getting shorter
white snow covers the land
while winter's breath runs cold
my heart gets warm again

heal
—

i fall in love so easily
overall quite rarely
yet if whole worlds within me merge
your heart so fast my home
i know where i find everything
feel comfortable and warm
yet sooner than i thought
my eyes wander outside

if you like me
please remind me
now and then
not to forget my world
come with me
get to know my home
question rather than judge
i will explain and i will show you
so you know well
where to find me
when i sometimes disappear

i fall in love so easily
my heart a place of warmth
i've learned
that maybe
will never be
enough for me

rome
—

you make me smile
on sad and happy days alike
never fooled
you know long before me
what i badly try to hide
quietly cleaning up my lies
wiping my eyes dry from dew
when i stumble you stand tall
whatever happens
i always know
you are here and tomorrow
the sun will rise for us
your love healed me
allowed new wounds
never lingering too long

i know today
through you
i found me

person
—

collecting our
delicate memories
like loose beads
on a thin thread

remembering
every breath
we shared
pancakes and
summer nights
naughty jokes
one blanket
future plans

i promise you
not a single moment
will i ever forget
from the first meeting
of our eyes
until the last time
in your arms

every second
will i hide
forever guard
deeply inside

iris
—

late august
impassively
drowning what's left of me
in sauvignon
faking a smile
when you arrive
i bite my lip
what a surprise
a man with spice

hello
bonjour

i am confused
how can i feel so drawn to you
while i am still
so caught in mourning

not biting my seduction
yourself a predator
you choose your prey
reading people in an instant
surely knowing when we met
in my weak state
i would've been an easy game

NOTE OF THANKS

Home is a very personal book and testimony to an intense and turbulent time of my life. Although I wrote most of my poetry silently for myself, it would never have come to life without the indispensable encouragement and support of a few people. First and foremost, I would like to thank Michelle Janssen, whose love of poetry made me want to share my poems in the first place almost a decade ago. Without her tireless attention, love for detail, and watchful eye, *Home* would still linger loosely in my old worn leather journal. Thank you for the countless hours, for every fine-tuning, for holding on when I had let go a long time ago. Thank you for always being my safe place, always understanding and never letting go. We all need people, who believe in us and make us believe in ourselves. I thank Matilda Halitaj and Theresa Schulz, my parents and my brother Felix for their constant encouragement, tireless support and the always open doors. I thank my father Niki for encouraging me to love the German language and my mother for never letting me forget my mother tongue. I always feel at home where you are. I thank my father Vlad for his widely awake thoughts, for the infusion of a never-ending longing that probably can be met only by the sound of his guitar. Also, Yury Kochnev, who decorated my youth with great literary works and kindled an unremitting passion for literature, art and theater. My charming German teacher, Dr. Barbara Sattler, who lives on in my memory like no other and knew how to lay the foundation for my love of German studies and history. I would like to thank my childhood friend Jannika Speer, whose gift of getting to the bottom of the human soul, asking the right questions, and hearing the unsaid, deeply shaped who I am today. A big thanks goes to the psychologist Jordan B. Peterson, whose work accompanied me in 2022 and shaped my thoughts and poetry. *descensus ad inferos* refers to his book Maps of Meaning, which along with his podcasts and lectures literally became a school of life to me. In a time when it doesn't seem easy to defend an opinion without being publicly denounced for its postulancy, I think it's even more important that we have people like Peterson, who have the courage and strength to stand up for their views, defend them against the most violent headwinds, and remind us what it means to be human. I would also like to thank the Argentinian author, psychiatrist and gestalt therapist Jorge Bucay. An artist of his kind, who knows how to weave the disciplines together in a delicate and sensitive way. All his works contributed to my inner journey and helped me to become more emphatic and look at occurrences from distinct perspectives. I warmly thank Dr. Christine Tabbert-Haugg for accompanying me on a wonderful journey of self-love and self-discovery. My spiritual teachers Rafa Valero, Raquel Sarojini Osório and Katalin Galbovy, whose mere presence calms my heart, and whose wisdoms remind me of what is important in life, helping me to distance myself from everything that I cannot influence. "We are sunny creatures, but sometimes it takes a storm", Raquel once said after a yoga class, getting to the heart of *Home*. Growth often hurts more than one might think at first. Change is frightening, but it is the only way we can peel off deeper layers, learn about ourselves and others and about life. Suffering and happiness together form a whole and are mutually dependent. Not suffering but apathy is the hell of present life. And sometimes you must stray from the path to see that you've been staggering in the dark for a while. At least I had to. From the bottom of my heart, I thank Jorge Torres, for so much. My wonderful friend Yves Belaine, who met me in the midst of a turbulent mess, yet with nothing but love, always managed to make me laugh and remind me of all the beauty there is in life. I thank Nicolas Czorny for our special bond, his unmistakable intuition, never ending French sarcasm and Pingui's little nudge that made me finish *Home* despite my decision not to. I thank everyone who has diverted me from my path. Everyone who had the courage to stand in my way. I thank all people who stand up for truth and authenticity, show feelings, allow vulnerability, forgive themselves and others and always choose love.

Sofia

ABOUT THE AUTHOR

Sofia has been writing since she remembers. Preferably about the little things in life everyone knows quite well. Unvarnished, quiet and loud questions of everyday life that concern our kind. What makes us who we are? What determines our purpose? Where does time fly, in its never ending hourglass. Does it stop and rest sometime or keep trickling away?

Home is her debut volume of poetry and tells of searching and finding, losing and longing, arriving and departing.

Printed by Amazon Italia Logistica S.r.l.
Torrazza Piemonte (TO), Italy